DINOSAUR JOKES

compiled by Laura Alden
illustrated by Russell Rigo

created by The Child's World

CHILDRENS PRESS, CHICAGO

Library of Congress Cataloging in Publication Data

Alden, Laura, 1955-
 Dinosaur jokes / compiled by Laura Alden ; illustrated by Russell Rigo ; created by The Child's World.
   p. cm.
 Summary: A collection of jokes, knock-knocks, and riddles about dinosaurs.
   ISBN 0-516-01865-5
   1. Dinosaurs—Juvenile literature. 2. Wit and humor, Junvenile.
 3. Riddles, Juvenile. 4. Knock-knock jokes. [1. Dinosaurs—Wit and humor. 2. Knock-knock jokes. 3. Jokes. 4. Riddles.]
 I. Rigo, Russell, ill. II. Title.
 PN6231.D65A44   1988   88-17489
 818'.5402—dc19   CIP
                                                              AC

Copyright © 1988 by Regensteiner Publishing Enterprises, Inc.
All rights reserved. Published simultaneously in Canada.
Printed in the United States of America.

 2 3 4 5 6 7 8 9 10 11 12 R 95 94 93 92 91 90 89

TABLE OF CONTENTS

Dinosaur Who?
  (Knock-knocks about Dinosaurs) 4
Riddled with Dinosaurs
  (Riddles about Dinosaurs) 12
The Biggest Joke of All
  (Jokes about Dinosaurs) 26

Dinosaur Who?

Knock-knock.
Who's there?
Ida.
Ida who?
Ida love to have a pet dinosaur.

Knock-knock.
Who's there?
Dish.
Dish who?
Dish little dinosaur went to market....

Knock-knock.
Who's there?
Dinosaur.
Dinosaur who?
Dinosaur from playing too much baseball.

Knock-knock.
Who's there?
Brachiosaurus.
Brachiosaurus who?
Brachiosaurus break the window.

Knock-knock.
Who's there?
Howard.
Howard who?
Howard you like to ride a dinosaur?

Knock-knock.
Who's there?
Dino.
Dino who?
This joke is dino-mite!

Knock-knock.
Who's there?
Eileen.
Eileen who?
Eileen out of the way when a dinosaur walks by.

Knock-knock.
Who's there?
Tyrannosaurus rex.
Tyrannosaurus rex who?
Tyrannosaurus rex everything!

Knock-knock.
Who's there?
Irish.
Irish who?
Irish I'd see a dinosaur.

Knock-knock.
Who's there?
Thumping.
Thumping who?
Thumping tall, green, and slimy behind you!

Knock-knock.
Who's there?
Where.
Where who?
Where, oh where have the dinosaurs gone?

Knock-knock.
Who's there?
Ron.
Ron who?
Ron! There's a dinosaur coming!

Knock-knock.
Who's there?
Mai.
Mai who?
This is Mai dinosaur.

Knock-knock.
Who's there?
Spell.
Spell who?
Spell Tyrannosaurus and I won't tell any more knock-knock jokes.

Knock-knock.
Who's there?
Ben.
Ben who?
Ben looking for that dinosaur!

Knock-knock.
Who's there?
Butternut.
Butternut who?
Butternut let that dinosaur get any closer!

Knock-knock.
Who's there?
Hominy.
Hominy who?
Hominy years ago did the dinosaurs live?

Knock-knock.
Who's there?
Kenya.
Kenya who?
Kenya imagine how big Brachiosaurus was?

Knock-knock.
Who's there?
Icey.
Icey who?
Icey a dinosaur over there!

Knock-knock.
Who's there?
Plateosaurus.
Plateosaurus who?
Clean your Plateosaurus.

Knock-knock.
Who's there?
Adam.
Adam who?
Adam my way, a dinosaur is coming!

Knock-knock.
Who's there?
Derision.
Derision who?
Derision room in this world for dinosaurs anymore.

Knock-knock.
Who's there?
Passion.
Passion who?
Passion by looking for a dinosaur.

Knock-knock.
Who's there?
Roman.
Roman who?
Roman around looking for dinosaurs.

Knock-knock.
Who's there?
Virus.
Virus who?
Virus you always telling these dinosaur jokes?

Knock-knock.
Who's there?
Achilles.
Achilles who?
Achilles dinosaur jokes.

Knock-knock.
Who's there?
Addis.
Addis who?
Addis no way to treat an old dinosaur.

Knock-knock.
Who's there?
B.C.
B.C. who?
B.C.'ing you!

Riddled With Dinosaurs

What do dinosaurs have that no other animal has?
Baby dinosaurs.

How do you talk to a dinosaur?
Use big words.

How many dinosaurs can fit into an empty box?
One. After that, it is not empty.

Which will burn longer—the candles on the birthday cake of a five-year-old dinosaur or the candles on the birthday cake of a six-year-old dinosaur?
Neither. No candles burn longer; they all burn shorter.

How can you tell when there's a dinosaur in the dryer?
The door won't shut.

How do you make a statue of a dinosaur?
Get a big piece of stone and cut away everything that does not look like a dinosaur.

What makes little dinosaurs go into a cave?
Their den-mothers.

How long should a dinosaur go without water?
Until it gets thirsty.

How do you make a dinosaur float?
Add two scoops of ice cream and one dinosaur to one quart of root beer.

If trains run on train tracks and cars run on race tracks, what do dinosaurs run on?
Their feet.

How do you get down off a dinosaur?
You don't get down off a dinosaur; you get it off a goose.

What is grey, has four legs, and a trunk?
A Brontosaurus on vacation.

When can three big dinosaurs go out under one tiny umbrella and not get wet?
When it is not raining.

What kind of dinosaur can jump higher than a house?
All kinds. Houses can't jump.

What are the four animals in the dinosaur family?
The mother dinosaur, the father dinosaur, the son dinosaur, and the daughter dinosaur.

Why did the dinosaur stand on his head?
To trip the birds.

What did the magician say to the dinosaur?
"Hocus, pocus, Diplodocus!"

What weighs 500 million pounds and sticks to the roof of your mouth?
A peanut butter and Brontosaurus sandwich.

Do you know why dinosaurs never forget?
No one ever tells them anything.

What does a 60-foot tall Tyrannosaurus eat?
Anything he wants.

Why do dinosaurs have such a great sense of humor?
They have enormous funny bones!

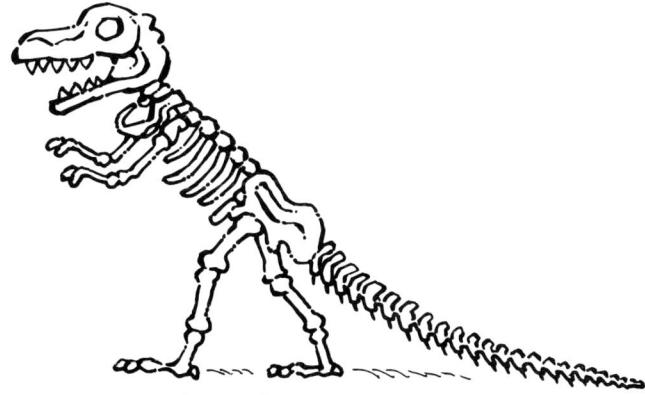

What do you do with a blue dinosaur?
Cheer him up!

How does a dinosaur get up a tree?
Climbs on an acorn and waits.

Why did the dinosaur paint her toenails red?
So she could hide in the strawberry patch.

What do you call a three-ton dinosaur?
"Sir."

Who won the dinosaur beauty contest?
Nobody.

How does a dinosaur get down from a tree?
He sits on a leaf and waits for the fall.

How can you tell when a dinosaur has been in the refrigerator?
There are footprints in the butter.

How can you tell a baby boy dinosaur from a baby girl dinosaur?
One is wrapped in blue and the other in pink.

Why did the dinosaur climb to the top of the skyscraper?
Because he didn't fit into the elevator.

Can you tell me how long dinosaurs should be fed?
The same as short dinosaurs.

Why did the Brontosaurus have such a long neck?
Because his head was so far from his body.

What is the best thing to do when you find a dinosaur in your bed?
Find somewhere else to sleep.

What do you have to know to teach a dinosaur tricks?
More than the dinosaur.

What time would it be if five dinosaurs were chasing you?
Five after one.

What did Tyrannosaurus say when he saw a caveman?
"I'd like to get to gnaw you."

What happened to the dinosaur that took the five o'clock train home?
He had to give it back.

What did the dinosaur think when the caveman caught her by the tail?
"That's the end of me!"

Why should a dinosaur always be a hungry person's best friend?
Because he's sure to give you a bite.

What's the difference between a strawberry and a dinosaur?
A strawberry is red.

What's the first thing the dinosaur put in the garden?
His feet.

Why did dinosaurs live in jungles?
They were too big to live in houses.

What does a dinosaur become after it is one year old?
Two years old.

What kind of dinosaur sees as much in the rear as he does in the front?
A blind one.

How did the dinosaur feel after he had eaten a whole pillow?
Down in the mouth.

When is a dinosaur most likely to enter a house?
When the door's open.

What did the caterpillar say when the Stegosaurus stepped on him?
Nothing.

Why are Brontosaurs slow to apologize?
It takes a long time for them to swallow their pride.

What do you get when you cross a hungry Tyrannosaurus with a saber-toothed tiger?
A Tyrannosaurus that is not hungry anymore.

How do you tell a dinosaur to hurry?
You say, "Shake a lego-saurus!"

When is a dinosaur's tail not a dinosaur's tail?
When it's a waggin' (wagon).

Andy: What was the dinosaur doing on Route 724?
Annie: About two miles an hour.

Why do dinosaurs go to bed?
Because the beds won't come to them.

Why do dinosaurs carry umbrellas?
Because umbrellas can't walk.

How do you divide three apples among five dinosaurs?
Make applesauce.

Why did the dinosaur chase his tail?
He was trying to make ends meet.

Why did the dinosaur go over the hill?
Because he couldn't go under the hill.

Where was the dinosaur when the lights went out?
In the dark.

What is the last thing a dinosaur takes off when she goes to bed?
Her feet off the floor.

Why do dinosaurs lie down?
They can't lie up.

What would you get if you crossed a dinosaur with a mouse?
Giant holes in your cheese.

Where do you put crying dinosaurs?
In the bawl park.

Why did the dinosaur turn around twice before he laid down?
He knew that one good turn deserved another.

How many dinosaurs does it take to make a leather coat?
None. Dinosaurs can't sew.

How can you tell when a dinosaur is a superstar?
He wears dark glasses.

Why do dinosaurs eat raw meat?
Because they can't cook.

How does a dinosaur add and subtract?
With a calculator.

What do you call a dinosaur who gets 60% of the vote?
President.

Why did the dinosaur scratch herself?
She was the only one who knew where it itched.

What do you call a dinosaur who crosses the desert?
Sandy Claws.

What plant eats a ton of meat all at once?
A Venus-dinosaur trap.

How much fur can you get from a dinosaur?
As fur as you can get.

What did the cavewoman do when she found a dinosaur chewing on her dictionary?
She took the words right out of his mouth.

What do you get if you cross a dinosaur with Billy the Kid?
A dinolaw.

What do you get if you cross a dinosaur with an ice house?
A dinoloo.

The Biggest Joke of All

Caveman: Where do baby dinosaurs come from?
Cavewoman: BIG storks!

Cavewoman: What do you do when a dinosaur sneezes?
Caveman: Get out of the way!

Dino: What does a dinosaur do to keep from dying?
Dinah: He goes into the living room.

Girl: Did you know that millions of years ago dinosaurs roamed the earth?
Boy: Couldn't they find a safe neighborhood?

Dino: What is the best way to talk to a dinosaur?
Dinah: Long distance!

Annie: They have lots of old dinosaur bones in the museum.
Andy: How come? Can't they afford the new ones?

Caveboy: What should you say if you meet a two-headed dinosaur?
Cavegirl: Hello! Hello!

Annie: How does a two-headed dinosaur talk?
Andy: In double talk.

Boy: What would a dinosaur who ate his mother's sister be called?
Girl: An aunt eater.

Annie: What's worse than a snake with a sore belly?
Andy: A Brontosaurus with a sore throat!

Boy: I'd like a quarter's worth of dinosaur seed please.
Shopkeeper: How many dinosaurs do you have?
Boy: None, but I want to grow some.

Cavegirl: Look at that bunch of dinosaurs.
Caveboy: Not bunch, herd.
Cavegirl: Heard what?
Caveboy: Herd of dinosaurs.
Cavegirl: Sure, I've heard of dinosaurs.
Caveboy: No, a dinosaur herd.
Cavegirl: Why should I care what a dinosaur heard? Good-bye!

Dino: What did the caveman say when he slid down the dinosaur's neck?
Dinah: "So long!"

**Mother dinosaur
to baby dinosaur:** What are you doing?
Baby dinosaur: I'm chasing a caveman.
Mother dinosaur: How often do I have to tell you not to play with your food?

Dinah: How did Tyrannosaurus rex like his steak?
Dino: Medium roar.

Girl: How do you shoot a blue dinosaur?
Boy: I don't know.
Girl: With a blue gun. And how do you shoot a white dinosaur?
Boy: With a white gun?
Girl: No. You hold his nose until he turns blue and then shoot him with the blue gun.

Boy: Is it true that a dinosaur won't attack you if you carry a flashlight?
Girl: That depends on how fast you carry it!

Dinah: I wish I had enough money to buy a dinosaur.
Dino: What would you do with a dinosaur?
Dinah: Who wants a dinosaur? I just want the money.

Cavewoman: I bet you can't guess how many dinosaurs are standing just outside our cave!
Caveman: One hundred and seven.
Cavewoman: How did you know?
Caveman: I just counted the legs and divided by four.

Annie: What are you painting, Andy?
Andy: A picture of a Brontosaurus, eating grass.
Annie: Where's the grass?
Andy: The Brontosaurus ate it.
Annie: Where's the Brontosaurus?
Andy: Why should it stay around when all the grass is gone?

Cavegirl: Wow! Who stepped on your foot?
Caveboy: See that Stegosaurus over there?
Cavegirl: Yes.
Caveboy: Well, I didn't.

Caveman: What's the plural of lion?
Cavewoman: Lions.
Caveman: Right. What's the plural of mouse?
Cavewoman: Mice.
Caveman: Right. And what's the plural of Tyrannosaurus rex?
Cavewoman: Who would want more than one of those?

Patient: Can a person be in love with a dinosaur?
Doctor: No.
Patient: Oh, well. Do you know anyone who wants to buy a very large engagement ring?

Annie: What's the difference between a dinosaur and a mattababy?
Andy: What's a "mattababy?"
Annie: Nothing, dear. What's the matter with you?

Caveboy: I can lift a dinosaur with one hand.
Cavegirl: I don't believe you.
Caveboy: Get me a dinosaur with one hand and I'll prove it.

Dino: I lost my pet dinosaur!
Dinah: Have you put an ad in the paper?
Dino: What good would that do? He can't read!

Boy: What would you say if I showed you a dinosaur head on a ten-cent piece?
Girl: Dimes have changed.

Andy: What would you get if you crossed a witch with a dinosaur?
Annie: I don't know, but she would need an awfully big broomstick!

Two cavemen were out hunting and gathering when a Tyrannosaurus rex appeared in front of them.

"Keep calm," said the first caveman. "Remember that book we read about dinosaurs? It said if you stand still and look the dinosaur right in the eye, he will turn around and run."

"Yeah," said the second caveman. "You read the book and I read the book, but has *he* read the book?"

Cavegirl to friend: Don't be afraid. Our pet dinosaur will eat off your hand.
Friend: That's what I'm afraid of!

Little Caveboy: I'd like to buy a baby dinosaur, please. How much do they cost?
Store Owner: Ten dollars apiece.
Little Caveboy: How much does a whole one cost?

Mother dinosaur: This seems like a good place for a picnic.
Father dinosaur: It must be. Fifty million flies can't be wrong.

Cavewoman to daughter: If you were by yourself and a dinosaur charged you, what would you do?
Daughter: Pay him.

Dinah's pet dinosaur died and Dinah's father sat beside its big body in tears.

"There, there," said a neighbor from the next cave. "I know a pet is like a member of the family and very dear to you, but..."

"*Dear* to me," Dinah's father interrupted. "Dear nothing! It's my job to *bury* the dumb thing!"

Annie: Why did the dinosaur cross the road?
Andy: She didn't. The chicken crossed the road.
Annie: Well, why did the chicken cross the road?
Andy: To get away from the dinosaur.

A woman came to visit her psychiatrist, leading a dinosaur.

"Doctor, I'm so worried about my husband," she said. "He thinks he's a dinosaur!"

Hungry Caveman: Waiter! There's a dead dinosaur in my soup.
Waiter: Yes, sir. It's the heat that kills them.

Visitor: I see there's a stuffed Tyrannosaurus' head in your uncle's den.
Caveboy: Yes, my uncle spent several years hunting for one.
Visitor: What is it stuffed with?
Caveboy: My uncle. He finally found one.

Dino: How can you tell when there's a dinosaur under your bed?
Dinah: Everyone knows that. When your nose hits the ceiling!

Girl: Did you know there once was a dinosaur with six legs?
Boy: Really?
Girl: Yup. He had forelegs in front and two legs behind.

Andy: Which would you rather have—a Tyrannosaurus eat you or a saber-toothed tiger?
Annie: I'd rather have the Tyrannosaurus eat the tiger, thanks!

Cavegirl: What's the difference between a dinosaur and a flea?
Caveboy: A dinosaur can have a flea, but a flea can't have a dinosaur.

First dinosaur: What's that book you're reading?
Second dinosaur: It's called *How to Serve Your Fellow Man.*

Caveboy: Why do dinosaurs wear slippers?
Cavegirl: So they can sneak up behind caveboys!

Caveman: Come right in, my friend.
Nervous guest: Well, does that dinosaur bite?
Caveman: That's what I want to find out. I only got her this morning.

Dinah: What makes more noise than a dinosaur caught in a trap?
Dino: Two dinosaurs!

Cavewoman: Will my Brontosaurus get a sore throat if she gets her feet wet?
Dinosaur Specialist: Yes, but not until the following week.

Caveman: How can you tell a dinosaur from spaghetti?
Cavewoman: The dinosaur doesn't slip off of your fork.

Dino: Why did the dinosaur's grandmother knit him five socks?
Dinah: She heard he grew another foot.

Father dinosaur: What are you going to be when you grow up?
Son dinosaur: I'm going to join the circus and be a midget.
Father dinosaur: Don't be silly. Dinosaurs are much too big to be midgets.
Son dinosaur: That's okay. I'll be the biggest midget in the world!

Boy dinosaur: Did you hear that the old one-eyed dinosaur finally closed her school?
Girl dinosaur: No, why did she?
Boy dinosaur: She only had one pupil.

Andy: How can you tell if a dinosaur has been drinking your tomato juice?
Angie: By the teeth marks on the can.

Andy: Why was the Tyrannosaurus rex a great artist?
Annie: A great artist?
Andy: Sure. He could draw blood.

Annie: Why did Noah just let two dinosaurs into the ark?
Andy: I have no idea.
Annie: He was only preserving pairs.

Boy: Why was the dinosaur afraid to go near the ocean?
Girl: He knew there was something fishy about it.

Caveboy: What are you doing?
Cavegirl: I'm feeding half of my peanuts to the dinosaurs.
Caveboy: That's nice of you.
Cavegirl: Yeah. Dinosaurs love peanut shells!

Older Stegosaurus: Did you take a bath today?
Younger Stegosaurus: No, why? Is there one missing?

Dinah: What's in the middle of dinosaurs?
Dino: Their stomachs?
Dinah: No, no. The letter s!

Boy: Why did the dinosaur brush his teeth?
Girl: To prevent dinosaur breath.

Cavewoman: Is this the local health office?
Health Officer: Yes. May I help you?
Cavewoman: I live with my three brothers and one of them keeps a Tyrannosaurus rex in our cave.
Health Officer: Yes?
Cavewoman: The other keeps six Brontosaurs and the third has ten Triceratops that he never lets out. The air is terrible and the smell is unbearable.
Health Officer: Why don't you open the door and let in some air?
Cavewoman: And let my fifteen Pteradactyls escape?

Caveboy: I'm taking my pet dinosaur to the dentist.
Cavegirl: Whatever for?
Caveboy: To improve his bite.

Dinah: Why did the dinosaur go to the library?
Dino: I know! She needed to bone up on a few things.

What do you get if a dinosaur walks through a strawberry patch?
Strawberry jam.

Annie: Do you know what the dinosaurs' holiday is?
Andy: The dinosaurs are all dead!
Annie: Right. That's why their holiday is Memorial Day.

Dino: Where do dinosaurs get their mail?
Dinah: Where do you think? At the dead letter office!

Caveboy: Why do dinosaurs enjoy people who get hot under the collar?
Cavegirl: I don't know, why?
Caveboy: They occasionally like a warm meal.

Dinah: What did the boy dinosaur say to the girl dinosaur?
Dino: How about, "I like your blood type?"
Dinah: That's "A positive!"

Cavegirl: I've been invited to a dinosaur's birthday party. What should I say?
Mother: Wish him a happy birthday!

Andy: Did you know that there is still a place where you can find dinosaurs?
Annie: Where?
Andy: In the dictionary.

Boy: Who is the most famous dinosaur doctor?
Girl: I don't know. I didn't know dinosaurs could be doctors.

Sister dinosaur: Why is your leg in a cast?
Brother dinosaur: I broke it in three places.
Sister dinosaur: If I were you, I wouldn't go to those places anymore.

Girl: What did the baby dinosaur want for Christmas?
Boy: Juth what I want—my two front teef!

What's as large as a dinosaur but weighs nothing?
Its shadow.

Why did the dinosaur paint his toenails different colors?
So he could hide in the Easter Basket.

What has eight legs and goes slurp, slurp, slurp?
Two dinosaurs drinking sodas.

What was the quickest dinosaur called?
The prontosaurus.

Why don't dinosaurs worry about being weighed?
Their scales are always with them.

Why were dinosaurs wrinkled?
They were too big to iron.

What's red, huge, and hates to be touched?
  A dinosaur with a sunburn.

What has a long neck, sunglasses, and polka-dot shorts?
  A dinosaur on vacation.

Dino: Did I ever tell you about the time I came face to face with a meat-eating dinosaur?
Dinah: No! What happened?
Dino: The dinosaur stared at me and I stared at the dinosaur. He started coming closer. . . and closer. . .and closer. . .
Dinah: Yikes! What did you do?
Dino: I closed the book!